"S T Kimbrough's poems create a vision of our world that is captivating. Some poems help all of us to develop 'the poetic imagination' that is the goal of all erudition."

—JAMES H. CHARLESWORTH,
President, Foundation on Judaism and Christian Origins

"For decades, S T Kimbrough has been teaching us that much of the Christian faith is better sung than said, relished rather than reasoned. In this fine collection of his poems, S T shows us the beauty in believing as well as the faith that admits to doubts and tensions within our faith. Wise, cheerful, hopeful, and full of delight, S T's poems are a gift to any of us who believe but need help to persist in our believing."

—WILL WILLIMON,
Duke Divinity School

"S T Kimbrough brings his truly diverse talents and interests into poems which probe our daily concerns, worries, and doubts and provide us with psalm-like redemptive verse. His and William Lawrence's introductions guide readers onto pathways through and out of our personal and social traumas."

—RUSSELL E. RICHEY,
Candler School of Theology, emeritus

"S T Kimbrough's poetry amply illustrates his long engagement with Methodist hymnody, the rhythms of which infuse these poems. They are rooted as well in Wesleyan theology, but with a clear eye to the struggles and doubts of contemporary Christians. It is a fusion that draws the reader into a sense of worship, which is at one with Kimbrough's lifelong work."

—Robert Hunt,
Perkins School of Theology, Southern Methodist University

"Is there any book more pertinent in terrifyingly tumultuous times than one that helps us honestly wrestle with God? That relevance is the gift of S T Kimbrough's new collection of poems, *The Struggle to Believe*. In them we find the words to wade into a Jacob-like refusal to let go of the divine, even in the midst of great difficulties and doubt."

—Lester Ruth,
Duke Divinity School

The Struggle to Believe

The Struggle to Believe

Poems That Wrestle with Christian Truth

S T KIMBROUGH, JR.

Foreword by William B. Lawrence

RESOURCE *Publications* · Eugene, Oregon

THE STRUGGLE TO BELIEVE
Poems That Wrestle with Christian Truth

Copyright © 2022 S T Kimbrough, Jr. All rights reserved. Except for brief quotations in critical publications or reviews, no part of this book may be reproduced in any manner without prior written permission from the publisher. Write: Permissions, Wipf and Stock Publishers, 199 W. 8th Ave., Suite 3, Eugene, OR 97401.

Resource Publications
An Imprint of Wipf and Stock Publishers
199 W. 8th Ave., Suite 3
Eugene, OR 97401

www.wipfandstock.com

PAPERBACK ISBN: 978-1-6667-3310-5
HARDCOVER ISBN: 978-1-6667-2742-5
EBOOK ISBN: 978-1-6667-2743-2

DECEMBER 31, 2021 8:35 AM

Contents

Foreword by William B. Lawrence | vi

Introduction | x

Chapter 1
THE STRUGGLE TO BELIEVE
    Wrong-headed Faith | 3
    Faith? or Faith! | 4
    The Need of Grace | 6
    Grace | 7
    Forgiveness | 8
    Destiny | 9
    Pray? | 10
    Humility, Love, and Grace | 11

Chapter 2
THE STRUGGLE TO BELIEVE THE SCRIPTURES
    Owe Nothing but Love | 15
    No Partiality | 16
    Nothing New Under the Sun? | 17
    Shadrach, Meshach, Abednego | 19

Poor Man Lazarus | 20
Transformed Hearts of Stone | 21
Weak and/or Strong | 22
Life by Stealth | 23
Christ Brings Peace? | 24
What Did Jesus Say? | 25

Chapter 3
THE STRUGGLE TO BELIEVE IN THE INCARNATION

Incarnation | 29
A Refugee Savior | 30
A Gift at Christmas? | 32
A Holiday Spirit? | 33
As Jesus Grew from Boyhood | 34

Chapter 4
THE STRUGGLE TO BELIEVE IN CHRIST'S PASSION AND RESURRECTION

Christ's Passion | 37
If | 39
Lent | 40
A Lenten Prayer | 41
A Fast | 42
Sacrifice | 43
Dying Grace | 44
Trials and Conflicts | 45
Palm Sunday | 46
Good Friday | 47
Easter Faith | 48

Chapter 5
THE STRUGGLE TO BELIEVE IN THE MYSTERY

    At the Table | 51

    The Mystery of Bread and Wine | 52

    To Dine with Christ | 53

    Holy Sacrament and Word | 54

    O Holy Sacrament Divine | 55

    Word and Sacrament | 56

    "Remember Me" | 57

Chapter 6
THE STRUGGLE TO BELIEVE IN THE CHURCH

    Your Church? My Church? God's Church? | 61

    The Church? | 63

    The Church Is God's? | 64

    The Church without Walls? | 65

    Humility in the Church | 67

    A Church, A Mosque, A Synagogue | 68

    Unity—Disunity | 69

Foreword

IN HIS BOOK ON the twenty-eight Methodist ministers from Mississippi who challenged the closed society of The Methodist Church in the Magnolia State in 1963 with their published letter that called for an end to racial segregation, historian Joseph Reiff shares the experiences of the twenty-eight signers. One faced an angry parishioner, who demanded to know the biblical basis upon which his minister chose to endorse integration. As he prepared a list of relevant texts in the Bible, the minister received word from the member that he was not really interested in any such scriptural citations. "I don't want you to ruin the Bible for me," the member said.[1]

With this new book of poetry, S T Kimbrough steps into a similar situation. He helps believers express what many would rather not profess. Not every believer will admit it, but we struggle to believe what we affirm, and we struggle to trust texts that we claim as authoritative for it. Kimbrough gives us permission to acknowledge that we share the dreadful ambivalence of the parent with a seriously ill child, when that parent says to Jesus, "I have faith; help my lack of faith."[2] Through these verses, Kimbrough enables us to tell ourselves the truth. Faith is beautiful but with sharp edges. It is delicate but imparts strength when we practice it.

---

1. Joseph L. Reiff, *Born of Conviction: White Methodists and Mississippi's Closed Society* (New York: Oxford University Press, 2016), 131.

2. Mark 9:24 (*Common English Bible*).

His poems offer this glimpse of truth about religious people. We embrace the faith, but we struggle with it. We are committed to our beliefs as well as to the authoritative scriptures and creeds that undergird them, but we are skeptical about them. We cherish the Christmas story that tells of the incarnation of God in human flesh, but we have our suspicions about it. We rejoice at the resurrection story, but we wrestle with its reality. When we recite the creeds, we orally assert that we find them to be credible, but we are not credulous.

Faith is substantive, not superficial. It is driven by mystical purpose, not mere pretense. Therefore, the poetic and prosaic testimonies to faith must be delivered with the mysterious substance that is appropriate for the power to which they bear witness. The public forms with which faith is expressed must be consistent with the private feelings that faith embraces. In the poems that fill these pages, honesty prevails. And that is critically important for any religion. Its public face must match its private feeling. Its expression must match its intention. Its substance cannot tolerate superficial substitutes.

Kimbrough's verse addresses a world in which too many adherents of religion treat faith as a cloak in which they try to clothe their ideologies, ambitions, preferences, politics, pleasures, and successes. These poems display the truth about faith, directly and honestly. They shine anew a penetrating light on the fact that faith is not just a veneer of optimism or a gild of enthusiasm to make human life gleam. Faith is the power to confront and overcome fear, ignorance, injustice, oppression, bigotry, and all other forms of evil that are active forces of destruction. "Now faith is the substance of things hoped for, the evidence of things not seen," says the letter to the Hebrews (11:1, KJV). Faith is strong and powerful enough when facing destructive forces to deal with them, defy them, deny them, and defeat them. To use S T Kimbrough's word, faith is unafraid of "struggling" with truth, even when clinging to falsehood is more convenient.

As these poems acknowledge, spiritual seekers struggle to believe. Bible readers struggle to understand scripture. Theologians

Foreword

struggle to articulate church doctrine. Christians struggle to tolerate the imperfections of the church. Worshipers struggle with praying to a mysterious God. Sunday school teachers struggle to cope with the candid questions raised by children in classes. Ministers struggle with the problems posed to them by parents raising recalcitrant kids, couples considering divorce, and parishioners near the end of their lives on earth.

All believers struggle with the significance of the sacraments they celebrate. Anyone who has ever recited the church's creeds has struggled to make sense of their intellectual propositions regarding salvation. Everybody who has offered the Lord's Prayer has struggled to grasp the full significance of prayerfully requesting God's reign and God's will to thrive exactly the same "on earth as it is in heaven."

Two other aspects of Kimbrough's poetic gifts, contained and displayed in these pages, are important to note.

The first is that this is not a book for binge reading. It is not a spy novel, murder mystery, or how-to handbook that one should open and invest consecutive hours in devouring. It is most appropriately read in a meditative fashion, pouring over each poem multiple times, occasionally by reading the verses aloud and then in deep, undistracted silence. While the order in which its poems are collected is both intentional and important, it is not essential that one read only as a sequence of its printed pages. Every page will reveal new mysteries and reconcile old divisions. Kimbrough's book is best read prayerfully. It will strengthen the spirit for more struggles that lie ahead.

The second is that this is not to be dismissed as just a collection of poems. Methodists, none more thoroughly or completely than S T Kimbrough, treasure the doctrines and disciplines of faith equally in the forms of prose and poetry. John Wesley is best known for his published sermons, essays, books, and articles in prose. His brother Charles Wesley is best known for his hymns and poems. The Methodist movement was motivated, managed, and energized by both of their contributions. From their perspectives, Methodists did not just proclaim faith but also practiced it, and

Foreword

Methodists did not only propose theses about theology but also sang them.

Poetry, in short, is one of the original, traditional, and enduring vehicles for exploring, explaining, and expressing faith. So, this is a book that continues the Wesleyan style of being theologically engaged with the world.

Sometimes, Charles Wesley began a poetic piece with exuberant explosions of praise, like "Ye Servants of God, Your Master Proclaim!" Sometimes, he began with a beckoning to a spiritual encounter, like "Come, O Thou Traveler Unknown." Sometimes, he began with notes that grieved over the savagery and suffering that are all too present in the world, like "Our earth we now lament to see with floods of wickedness o'erflowed...." And, sometimes, he began with deeply difficult questions, like "And can it be that I should gain an interest in the Savior's blood? Died he for me, who caused his pain—For me, who him to death pursued?"

S T Kimbrough carries forward the founding legacy of Methodism. Ask hard questions. Struggle humbly. Be brave in believing personally and be bold in behaving publicly. And let a fine poet, whether an ancient psalmist or a current singer, help us continue to pray.

William B. Lawrence
Professor *Emeritus* of American Church History
Perkins School of Theology, Southern Methodist University

Introduction[3]

MOST PEOPLE OF FAITH struggle with aspects of their beliefs. These poems do not seek to propose resolutions to all faith struggles. They do seek to help us to examine ourselves and to be honest about these struggles and to know that to confront them does not mean to lose faith. Having studied and taught the biblical languages of Hebrew and Greek, and studied Aramaic, the language Jesus spoke, I am aware that there are not always simple solutions to many difficult linguistic problems in the Bible.

The first chapter begins with the subject of this book, namely, the struggle to believe. This by no means is a simple matter. Is it possible to have faith for the wrong reasons? Is faith our last resort when all else seems lost? What of helplessness and hopelessness? Can they open a window to faith understanding? The poem "Faith? or Faith!" stresses that we live by many things that we cannot see and we do not question their veracity: the rising and setting of the sun, the turning of the earth.

What does it mean to have faith in things that matter most, such as love of self and others? Can this faith be related to faith in the divine? Is it possible to have faith in unconditional love? This chapter also helps us to ask questions about the meaning of grace, forgiveness, and destiny, subjects with which many people struggle every day. How do these concepts affect the growth and reality of faith?

---

3. The English translation of all biblical passages throughout this book are from the *New Revised Standard Version of the Bible*.

INTRODUCTION

If we have no room for grace,
   are not kind to the unkind,
our lives leave no single trace,
   we're out of sight, out of mind.

But there is an ongoing struggle to find room for grace.
   How can we know there's grace
   among the human race,
   when kindness is a word
   that many find absurd.

Nevertheless, the struggle to believe is quite normal, or we may not *think* about faith at all. To ask the lasting and burning questions about belief does not mean we have lost faith, are losing it, or will lose it. It should indicate the fervent desire for an authentic faith which willingly faces challenges and earnestly says with the father of a child in Mark's Gospel: "I believe; help my unbelief!" (Mark 9:24).

It is glaringly apparent that people do not always respond positively to many admonitions of Holy Scripture. Even if they do not openly struggle with them, through silence they may simply avoid them. In chapter 2, I look at a few biblical passages with which some folks struggle today, even if they are unaware. In Romans 13:8 we are admonished, "Owe no one anything, except to love one another." Clearly the response of many Christians is anything but love for the other. Denominations and divisions within them make this struggle obvious.

In Acts 10:34 one reads the words of Peter, "I truly understand that God shows no partiality." If we are to personify God's nature, namely love, how can we be partial to someone or to a particular group of people. Yet, threads of racism throughout world cultures suggest that many who believe in the truths of Holy Scripture cannot abide by them. Partiality is rampant throughout the world.

How shall one reconcile the passage from Ecclesiastes 1:9 that affirms "there is nothing new under the sun" with the affirmation of the one who sits on the throne in Revelation 21:5, "See, I am making all things new"? Need one struggle with the reconciliation of these different statements? Yes, indeed, if one believes that Jesus' advent, ministry, and resurrection open a new way for humankind.

INTRODUCTION

Other poems in chapter 2 address admonitions about miracles, the story of a man after death, and a theological-surgical operation that the prophet Ezekiel avers can be performed on all, namely to remove hearts of stone in people and to replace them with hearts of flesh, that is, hearts that are warm, alive, and beating. The poem "Transformed Hearts of Stone" treats this ongoing struggle in human nature of how to replace hearts of stone with living hearts.

Many commentators have struggled with the Pauline statement in 2 Corinthians 12:9, "My grace is sufficient for you, for [my] power is made perfect in weakness." How easily one may say that in every circumstance God's grace is sufficient and thereby one's power is made perfect in weakness. These words in themselves express the lifelong struggle to trust in such an affirmation.

Chapter three concerns what is considered to be a stumbling block for many in the history of the Christian faith, namely, the Incarnation of God in Christ. People have wrestled for centuries with the God-child revelation. Could understanding Jesus as "A [Jewish] Refugee Savior" assist the human grasp of the Incarnation's meaning?

> A Savior, once a refugee,
>   a fugitive from evil's grasp,
> knew well oppressed folk must be free,
>   who for the breath of freedom gasp.

It is one thing to speak of the gift of love in the Incarnation, but one struggles to reconcile the behavior of those who embrace it with their unloving words and acts.

There is also the puzzle of the wisdom of Jesus, which the Jewish elders of his time struggled to accept.

Introduction

> When elders in the Temple heard
> > him answer questions there one day,
> they were surprised how wise each word.
> > Could this boy teach teachers to pray?
>
> That they should learn from one so young,
> > was not the elders' usual way.
> The wisdom they heard from his tongue
> > one still is studying today.

Chapter 4 addresses yet another stumbling block through the centuries for Christian belief, namely, the week of Christ's passion and his subsequent crucifixion, burial, and resurrection. Suffering for the sake of peace and goodwill is sometimes labeled a "martyr complex." In what sense does Christ's suffering and persecution mirror the lives of people throughout the world, even today? Is there something in the "cruciform life" that shows us how all humankind should live? Perhaps this is a persistent struggle for Christians.

The poem "If" stirs one's imagination about how one might deal with the sensitive situation Jesus' disciples faced with him in the Garden of Gethsemane. While we do not need to play psychological games, imagination is often a worthy means of interpreting the Scriptures, especially when we are examining how we might respond to life situations that emerge within them. This is extremely important for Christians since we spend the Christian year exploring how to respond to diverse aspects of Christ's life. For example,

> For Easter we cannot prepare,
> > if there's no time apart.
> In quiet we become aware
> > what motivates the heart,
>
> what motivates the heart to sing
> > an alleluia Easter morn.
> No look within, a tragic thing:
> > there miracles are born.

INTRODUCTION

For this reason in "A Lenten Prayer," "I pray for openness to see / a sacrificial depth in me."

> If thus the forty days be spent
> I never will forget this Lent.

In the struggle to understand the New Testament affirmation that "Christ has suffered once for all"—

> Most surely this can never mean
>   an end to human suffering,
> but from Christ's passion we may glean
>   the impact of his offering.
> Christ's passion shows life cruciform
>   how humankind should live and be,
> the gift of self becomes the norm,
>   until a better world we see.

Thus, the poems in this chapter explore the events of the Passion Week until one comes to the moments of Christ's death upon a cross. Is the question here really that the honor of God is challenged and that the crucifixion dishonors God?

> And so, it was upon the cross
>   two words there came alive:
> *forgive* and *love,* our gain not loss,
>   through them we may survive.

The resurrection of Jesus remains a stumbling block for many, and many believing Christians still struggle with the veracity of this New Testament event.

> "How could it be that Christ arose?"
>   some ask with good intent.
> They probe the doctrines they oppose:
>   with doubts sincerely meant.

Introduction

> Yet, hope lives on that Christ arose,
> in each believing soul,
> and sacrificial love us shows
> the faith that makes us whole.
>
> If Easter faith we would possess,
> let doubts each year depart;
> self-giving love let us profess
> in every beating heart.

Chapter 5 addresses the struggle to believe in the mystery of the Eucharist. How is it possible that we are transformed by the bread and wine, the body and blood of Christ? The poem "At the Table" avers "Transformed we are who here will dine / on love, found here in bread and wine." Love is the key above all else. Just as the New Testament affirms that "God is love," so it is that the bread and wine are the elements of love to be shared with all people. This is the table of God's love: "Thus at the table we will learn: / God's love within our hearts must burn!" This is both a mystery and a miracle.

> We who receive the bread and wine
> the mystery will know:
> for love transforms us as we dine,
> and as we rise and go.

Why does the poem "Holy Sacrament and Word" claim that "The eucharistic life's the sum / of all we in the church become"? It is because in the Eucharist love binds us together with one another across all boundaries. The church chooses thereby to be on the constant quest for God's nature, which is love. The Eucharist is the feast of love which binds together in God's love those who come to share in the feast.

Rather than struggling to prove each detail of the transformation of bread and wine, we should struggle to grasp the mystery and miracle of love shared in this meal and the personification of God's nature, i.e., love.

Introduction

The final chapter (6) of poems examines aspects of the meaning of the Christian church. Its diverse denominations clearly exhibit the struggles for centuries to attempt to define what the church *is* and which church *is* the church. Is there such a thing as an authentic Christian church: the eastern Orthodox Church(es), the Roman Catholic Church, the Protestant churches? The first three poems in this chapter affirm that the church belongs to God. It is not a denominational whipping post for members simply to do with as they please, though in many ways this is the way the church may appear to the world. Though one easily may condemn the struggle to discern church heretics in the middle ages, the ongoing break up and break off of new denominations stresses that some folk think there are still "disbelievers" from whom one needs to be separate.

> In brokenness, the church must pray:
> "Forgive our selfish thought.
> The church is God's, not ours to sway
> till it's with schism fraught."

I have no dream that many others will share my view of the church which attempts at least to be guided by a personification of God's nature, love. But I can draw no other conclusion from the Holy Scriptures except that the church is also to be a personification of love.

> A house of God should be a place,
> where no one seeks ill will,
> with doors wide open to each race
> where love each soul can fill.

Am I still struggling with many of the issues raised in these poems? Indeed I am. If the poetry in these pages provides the opportunity for others to share in these struggles openly and honestly, my words will have been wisely spent. Above all else, many of the struggles tend to disappear if one seeks, however feebly, to become a personification of God's nature, LOVE.

Chapter 1

The Struggle to Believe

WRONG-HEADED FAITH

What if there were no hope at all,
    and hopelessness our destiny,
and pointless life should us appall,
    and life become despondency?

What if there were nowhere to turn
    and kindness no one dared to show,
and sharing everyone should spurn,
    and speech should wound like a crossbow?

If faith alone's our last resort:
    and we say our God understands;
we will all goodness surely thwart,
    remove all goodness from our hands.

To say, "Don't worry, God knows best,
    and God will one day make things right,"
would sound as though we surely jest;
    such speech will our own faith indict.

If faith suggests our helplessness,
    what kind of God wants this result—
a realm of constant hopelessness
    where status quo is God's insult?

FAITH? OR FAITH!

We live by faith and not by sight,
    according to Saint Paul.
I wonder, do you think he's right?
    Does this apply to all?

This means, believe when we can't see,
    and is such faith then blind?
Belief in God all can't agree;
    some think it warps the mind.

And yet, we really live by faith
    in what we cannot see:
The earth will turn, the sun will rise,
    and love that's shown to me.

The order of the universe,
    is faith in it absurd?
And faith in God, is it perverse?
    by it are our thoughts blurred?

If we by faith should choose to live,
    by faith in the divine,
Will it determine what we give
    of selfless love, the sign?

The sign of all that matters most
    is selfless love for all.
Of this the selfless never boast.
    We learn this from Saint Paul.

Faith, hope, and love abide, these three,
    but love Paul boldly claims
is greatest and to life the key:
    the noblest of all aims.

THE NEED OF GRACE

What shall draw us together
    beyond the bounds of our race?
Though strong the ethnic tether,
    all must find the room for grace:

Room to say a gracious word,
    room to do a gracious deed,
room to listen, to be heard,
    room to help with human need.

If we have no room for grace,
    are not kind to the unkind,
our lives leave no single trace,
    we're out of sight, out of mind.

GRACE

How then shall grace abound
when kindness is not found,
where mercy is not known
and charity has flown?

How can we know there's grace
among the human race,
when kindness is a word
that many find absurd?

Grace gives, and gives, and gives,
and selfishness outlives.
Grace is an attitude,
a constant, joyous mood.

To live by grace means joy,
not a deceptive ploy.
Grace loves, does not condemn,
divides not "us" and "them."

Unconditional love,
yes, grace consists thereof.
Grace only can you know,
if love like this you show.

FORGIVENESS

Forgive, forgive, forgive, we're told,
but what if truth thereby were sold?
Forgiveness offers truth for sale,
if sincere words and trust both fail.

What can it mean—forgive, forgive—
completely free of grudge to live?
It means you never will forget:
you must forgive without regret.

Live free of grudges and regrets
while people worn with whines and frets
complain, complain at every turn,
and old resentments burn and burn?

The only remedy, Forgive!—
the only way for all to live!
It is a simple truth I own;
Is it a simple truth I've known!

DESTINY

Of kismet, destiny, called fate,
    to thwart it what's the chance?
Though sages centuries debate,
    does knowledge thus advance?

Some people try a Ouija board;
    a Talisman will do?
A prayer wheel or the prayers we hoard
    or prayers we always knew?

Can these decide what will transpire
    today, tomorrow too?
Some say the gods are not for hire
    and *que sera* will do.

Some do believe there's God's own will
    which cannot be defied.
It steers the course of good and ill
    no matter what is tried.

My preference is of God to think
    ill will is not God's choice.
Our freedom God prefers we link
    to goodwill, so rejoice.

PRAY?

On whom will you for strength depend,
yourself, your family, or a friend?
Is there a God who strength will lend?

Quite self-sufficient you would be
till unforeseen catastrophe
might rob you of sagacity.

How can serenity make wise
in moments of despair, surprise?
Will moments like these paralyze?

Is there nowhere that you can turn?
Will you with anguish seethe and burn
becoming withdrawn, taciturn?

Your soul let open wide to prayer,
even when to pray you might not dare,
even if you think no God is there.

Can prayer be the soul's wise resource,
as well as a mysterious force
that sets one on a wiser course?

You cannot know unless you pray;
yes, it's a most mysterious way,
a challenge for your soul to weigh.

HUMILITY, LOVE, AND GRACE

Humility, love, and grace,
three aspects of faith I trace,
and yet how rarely I find
the ones who keep them in mind.
Agape,* is it divine?
If so, how can it be mine?
Humility, virtue rare,
love and grace beyond compare.
One who lives life by these three,
learns *agape* one can be.

* Greco-Christian term for unconditional love: God's love for humankind and humankind's love for God.

Chapter 2

THE STRUGGLE TO BELIEVE THE SCRIPTURES

Romans 13:8, "Owe no one anything, except to love one another."

OWE NOTHING BUT LOVE

Owe nothing but love to another,
whether your father or your mother,
whether your sister or your brother.

Love others, yes, without exception.
Love others, yes, free of deception.
Love others with willful reception.

Love others, yes, at times that's hard work.
Love others, yes, at them do not smirk.
Love others, yes, love's work do not shirk.

Love does not do wrong to a neighbor,
love of neighbor should not be labor,
Then love lifelong, this gift you'll savor.

Acts 10:34, "Then Peter began to speak to them: 'I truly understand that God shows no partiality.'"

NO PARTIALITY

"God shows no partiality,"
    but who believes this true?
What of the stark reality:
    "We are the special few"?

So think some of one faith or race:
    think Christians, Muslims, Jews?
Legitimacy all can trace:
    each generation's news.

Can Sunni, Shia both be right?
    Reformed, Orthodox Jew?
And Christian churches, what a sight!
    How many? There's no clue!

If God shows no partiality,
    each faith and race must learn
a godly hospitality,
    intolerance to spurn.

Ecclesiastes 1:9, "What has been is what will be,
and what has been done is what will be,
and there is nothing new under the sun."

NOTHING NEW UNDER THE SUN?

If nothing's new under the sun,
    as Hebrew Scriptures say,
how then can Jesus be the one
    who offers a new way?

"Behold, I will make all things new,"
    the Scriptures' stunning claim,
but Koheleth, the preacher knew,
    he thought, things stay the same.

The Scriptures say God is the same,
    today and yesterday,
and Yahweh's the eternal name
    forever and for aye.

The constancy of the divine
    is Scripture's bold, stark view.
For this is there from God a sign?
    If we God's thoughts but knew!

From Genesis to its last book
    the Bible has one theme:
to open human eyes to look
    at God's plan to redeem.

But centuries came and centuries passed
    and humans could not see
their evil acts, turmoil amassed,
    had shaped their destiny.

So drastic was the earthly scene
    that even the divine
decided on a course pristine
    with hope hearts to incline.

Yes, something new under the sun
    omniscient God would plan,
the course of human history run:
    the advent of God-Man.

Yes, God old Koheleth defied
    and came to make things new,
and yet the old was not denied
    but seen from a new view.

The God-Man's name Emmanuel,
    "God with us" age to age,
makes new our lives—how long, how well—
    beyond the sacred page.

Book of Daniel, Chapter 3

SHADRACH, MESHACH, ABEDNEGO

Shadrach, Meshach, Abednego,
three men of history, long ago,
King Nebuchadnezzar defied.
The golden image at his side,
they would not worship, nor would kneel.
Were they just men with wills of steel?
The king then threatened death by fire,
for they had roused his kingly ire.
These men believed in God alone,
no golden image, kingly throne.
The king's command would not obey:
to bow and to an image pray.
The consequence was death by fire.
If not, the king would seem a liar.
Into the furnace they were cast,
and yet their faith was strong, steadfast.
When it was clear they had not died,
though they the king's command defied,
the king himself made a decree:
"The God of these men ours shall be.
No other god can show the way;
to other gods you shall not pray."
The story's point some like to think:
"Salvation," when life's on the brink!
The miracle is not the point,
though some this meaning would anoint.
The point is this: One God alone
deserves our faith, no golden clone.

Luke 16:22–25, "The poor man died and was carried away by the angels to be with Abraham. The rich man also died and was buried. In Hades, where he was being tormented, he looked up and saw Abraham with Lazarus by his side. He called out, 'Father Abraham, have mercy on me, and send Lazarus to dip his finger in water and cool my tongue; for I am in agony in these flames.' But Abraham said, 'Child, remember that during your lifetime you received your good things, and Lazarus in like manner evil things; but now he is comforted here and you are in agony.'"

POOR MAN LAZARUS

A poor man lay outside the gate
    before a rich man's home,
who feasted early, feasted late:
    food never ceased to come.

The poor man, Lazarus, sought crumbs
    that from the table fell.
"No, no!" the rich man said, which sums
    up life's sure path to hell.

In hell the rich man water pleads,
    but Abraham replies.
"No, Lazarus, can't meet your needs!
    Your greed all help denies."

Ezekiel 36:26, "A new heart I will give you, and a new spirit I will put within you; and I will remove from your body the heart of stone and give you a heart of flesh."

TRANSFORMED HEARTS OF STONE

The prophet, wise Ezekiel,
    who ages long since passed,
expressed a passion and a zeal,
    a hope we should hold fast:

That hearts of stone can be transformed
    from stone to hearts of flesh.
Such hearts with life are strangely warmed:
    God's Spirit makes them fresh.

Imagine our world with warmed hearts,
    inspired by Spirit divine!
When every burst of anger starts,
    warm hearts have a design:

A heart of flesh shares its embrace
    of eager, loving care
with every soul of every race;
    such hearts have love to spare.

Let us surrender anger, fear;
    let hearts fill with concern
to honor, love, care, *all* revere;
    goodwill for *all* to yearn.

All hearts made new by God's embrace,
    know not how, why, or when.
But all will know love leaves its trace,
    and all can start again.

2 Corinthians 12:9, "My grace is sufficient for you, for [my] power is made perfect in weakness."

WEAK AND/OR STRONG

"If I am weak, then I am strong,"
    averred th' Apostle Paul.
But could this paradox be wrong,
    or meaningless to all?

Is strength a virtue all folk need?
    You're taught you should be strong.
Make weakness then a lifelong creed:
    Be weak your whole life long?

Aren't opposites then weak and strong?
    How can the weak strong be?
Together strangely they belong
    didactic friends, you'll see.

The weak learn how they can be strong,
    the strong learn from the weak.
And mutually they get along,
    both can learn to be meek.

Luke 3:10, "And the crowds asked him, 'What then should we do?' In reply he said to them, 'Whoever has two coats must share with anyone who has none; and whoever has food must do likewise.'"

LIFE BY STEALTH

Whoever has two coats must share
    with those who have not one.
How can we then our hearts prepare
    and know if right we've done?

Keep no more than you truly need
    or you extort the poor.
A thought some wealthy rarely heed,
    lest they feel insecure.

Two coats, do they measure one's wealth?
    Yes, when the poor have none!
Refuse the gift, you live by stealth
    and needy persons shun.

Ephesians 2:13-14, 17, "But now in Christ Jesus you who were once far off have been brought near by the blood of Christ. For he is our peace; in his flesh he has made both groups into one and has broken down the dividing wall, that is, the hostility between us.
. . . So he came and proclaimed peace to you who were far off and peace to those who were near."

CHRIST BRINGS PEACE?

Do Christians think that Christ breaks down
    dividing walls, hostility
in every city, every town
    and brings in peace, civility?

Do Christians think that Christ brings peace
    to those far off and those who're near?
Do they divide without release
    and their divisions hold most dear?

Does not the world quite clearly see
    there's little faith that Christ brings peace,
if Christians act so differently
    and their divisions do not cease?

WHAT DID JESUS SAY?

If Jesus did not speak in Greek
    but Aramaic spoke,
some folk might offer the critique:
    Greek language is a cloak,

a cloak for what he really said,
    translation nuance lost.
For all who have the Gospels read
    is this the unknown cost?

One oft forgets his words to hear
    in other tongues or Greek,
to hear the wisdom of this seer,
    his counsel most unique!

The spirit of his words put first
    above each word for word;
for meaning have undying thirst,
    then Jesus you'll have heard.

Chapter 3

The Struggle to Believe in the Incarnation

INCARNATION

How can Christmas bring us joy
when illness could us destroy
our life and loved ones near us?
What is there that can cheer us?

It's hard to think far beyond
the ones of whom we are fond,
above all, our family
or friends that we like to see.

A Christmas with a virus
by no means is desirous.
The meaning of this season
gives life a special reason:

beyond ourselves new to see
there's more to life than just "we."
There's peace, goodwill, and wonder
and love a spell we're under.

A love, that's a mystery
that gives us a history
transcending ev'ry sorrow
with hope for each tomorrow.

This is an Incarnation,
a God-child revelation.

Matthew 2:13–15: Now after they had left, behold, an angel of the Lord appeared to Joseph in a dream and said, "Get up, take the child and his mother, and flee to Egypt, and remain there until I tell you; for Herod is about to search for the child, to destroy him." Then Joseph got up, took the child and his mother by night and went to Egypt and remained there until the death of Herod. This was to fulfill what had been spoken by the Lord through the prophet, "Out of Egypt I have called my son."

A REFUGEE SAVIOR

A Jewish boy from Palestine
    to Egypt with his parents fled,
for in a dream appeared a sign:
    King Herod wanted their child dead.

But when King Herod's time was passed,
    then Mary, Joseph, and their son
to Palestine returned at last;
    their time as refugees was done.

An immigrant, a refugee,
    the fate of this most holy child.
When you have lived such life you see
    the fate of half the world profiled.

Hosea, prophet wise, foretold,
    "From Egypt I have called my Son,"
Divine the summons and how bold:
    a refugee salvation won.

Salvation of the human race
    that seeks the least, the last, the lost
God's love will constantly embrace,
    embrace them all at any cost.

A Savior, once a refugee,
    a fugitive from evil's grasp,
knew well oppressed folk must be free,
    who for the breath of freedom gasp.

He's "born to set God's people free,"
    so wrote an eighteenth-century sage.*
Imagine this—a refugee
    is viewed as Savior age to age.

---

* Eighteenth-century poet-priest Charles Wesley: "Come, thou long-expected Jesus, / born to set thy people free."

A GIFT AT CHRISTMAS?

A special day called Christmas Eve
    comes 'round just once a year,
and children here and there believe
    that Santa brings them cheer.

The legend is, if good or bad
    one knows what to expect.
If bad, then you'll for sure be sad,
    for Santa you'll reject.

But Christmas Eve anticipates
    acceptance of us all,
and every child it celebrates—
    the good, bad, great or small.

So, children aren't called bad or good
    on every Christmas Eve,
for Christmas Day shows each child should
    the gift of love receive.

A HOLIDAY SPIRIT?

The spirit of the holidays,
    is there such a thing,
experienced in many ways,
    the way you carols sing?

The way art of Madonna, child
    might stop you, make you stare
and change your mood from sad to mild,
    invoke a sense of prayer.

The thrill of Christmas tree bright lights,
    an angel grandma made,
remind one of past years' delights;
    such feelings do not fade.

The spirit of the holidays,
    can it nostalgia be,
just what we feel in many ways,
    that moves emotionally?

Perhaps there's spirit in these things
    that yearly we relive;
perhaps this spirit does take wings
    and moves our hearts to give.

But Christmas spirit's mystery
    bears not nostalgia's sway;
it's love that lives eternally,
    love born on Christmas Day.

Luke 2:46–7: "After three days they found him in the temple, sitting among the teachers, listening to them and asking them questions. And all who heard him were amazed at his understanding and his answers."

AS JESUS GREW FROM BOYHOOD

As Jesus grew from boyhood on
    his father Joseph worked with wood.
Arriving daily with the dawn,
    young Jesus helped him as he could.

One wonders, did he woodcraft learn
    and play with toys that he had made,
then in the synagogue discern
    faith's meaning as the elders prayed.

When elders in the Temple heard
    him answer questions there one day,
they were surprised how wise each word.
    Could this boy teach teachers to pray?

That they should learn from one so young,
    was not the elders' usual way.
The wisdom they heard from his tongue
    one still is studying today.

Chapter 4

The Struggle to Believe in Christ's Passion and Resurrection

CHRIST'S PASSION

Why does one call it passion week?—
    remembering the suffering
of moments desperately bleak
    when death o'er Christ was hovering?
Though bearer of goodwill and peace,
    as sang the angels at his birth,
the cries of "Crucify" increase
    both then and now across the earth.

To suffer for peace and goodwill
    God offers to all humankind,
one should let Holy Week instill
    a lasting memory there to find
of those events in seven days
    that changed the course of history,
from songs of praise to evil ways
    that led to cross-borne Calvary.

That God should suffer, some object,
    and see not that the power divine
through suffering evil did reject,
    the suffering in your life and mine.
To understand Christ's suffering there
    outside Jerusalem's city wall
will mirror suffering everywhere,
    for Christ has suffered once, for all.

Most surely this can never mean
    an end to human suffering,
but from Christ's passion we may glean
    the impact of his offering.
Christ's passion shows life cruciform
    is how all humankind should live;
the gift of self becomes the norm,
    for this is what all have to give.

IF

If I were one to suffer there
    in dark Gethsemane,
I am not sure within my heart
    just what my prayer would be.

If I had had to be alone,
    and face the Master's lot,
I do not know if I'd have been
    prepared to face the plot.

If my close friends in this dark hour
    had fallen fast asleep,
would I have felt my faith so strong
    or cast into the deep?

If I'd been asked by Christ himself
    "Will you stand watch one hour?"
Like Simon Peter, James, and John,
    would I have lacked the power?

I do not know how to respond,
    and I will never know
how in the garden I'd behaved
    those centuries ago.

LENT

During the forty days of Lent
    reflection is one's goal.
In inward quests long hours are spent
    to search deep in one's soul.

Like Jesus in the wilderness,
    in quietude alone,
we find there is no emptiness,
    though emptiness we've known.

Our emptiness, a stark contrast
    to God's fulfilling grace
of Easter love, so rich and vast,
    within will find no place.

For Easter we cannot prepare,
    if there's no time apart.
In quiet we become aware
    what motivates the heart,

what motivates the heart to sing
    an alleluia Easter morn.
No look within, a tragic thing:
    there miracles are born.

A LENTEN PRAYER

For forty days of Lent I pray
my deepest anguish to allay;
the anguish that in me may rise,
when shallow thoughts I may devise
to shield me from bold honesty
and lack of faithful constancy;
the constancy to stand by friends
with neighbor-love that knows no ends.
I pray for openness to see
a sacrificial depth in me.
O God, direct my intellect—
my mind, my thoughts that I expect
to live with humble modesty,
to love all others consciously.
Remove from me all prejudice;
and save me from the precipice
of selfish, blind, immured concern.
Teach me for others' needs to yearn.
If thus the forty days be spent,
I never will forget this Lent.

A FAST

A fast and self-denial
we oft view as a trial.
Self-discipline oft purges
the body's wrong-bent urges.
Fast and learn humility.
Fast and shed hostility.
Fast when we face what's unjust.
Fast to foster renewed trust.
To loose chains of oppression,
each fast's an intercession.
Each fast is a sincere prayer
that makes us much more aware
of others, self, God each day;
this is why with fasts we pray.

SACRIFICE

In passion week of sacrifice
we know, that suffering won't suffice.
To suffer is not sacrifice,
Christ's sacrifice is more precise.
To sacrifice the self, one gives,
shown by the love through which one lives.
Christ's sacrifice upon the cross
did not stress merely one life's loss.
Christ's sacrifice injustice spurned:
forgiveness in its place is learned.
Thus sacrifice is victory
of love throughout world history.
Where sin, false accusations, reign,
the gift of self, love will sustain.
Forgiveness is Christ's passion word
which from the cross is always heard.
Forgive, they know not what they do:
Forgiveness is Christ's new worldview.
*This passion message is for all,
hence be forgiving, heed its call.*

DYING GRACE

We sense once more at Lent God's grace
    revealed in sacrifice,
and learn, astounded, to embrace
    God's own immortal price.

We learn to prize the life grace gives
    through God's begotten Son;
we learn that grace his death outlives;
    grace has new life begun.

Why should God's grace for us then die?
    Are we worth such a price?
In death grace shows the reason why
    it outlives sacrifice.

Grace dying on a cross for us
    seems such a strange wrought scene;
yet, in self-giving it is thus
    we learn what life should mean.

TRIALS AND CONFLICTS

Can I be free of every trial
    before I earth depart?
Is this reality's denial,
    deception of the heart?

Your trials always let you know
    that you're indeed alive,
for without conflict there's no flow
    to life for which to strive.

You know what's good, you know what's bad;
    a storm contrasts the calm,
and happy's opposite of sad,
    for sick souls there is balm.

While trials aren't your favorite thing
    to live with every day,
if positive, your thoughts, their sting
    may slowly fade away.

No, without trials I will not live;
    resolve them I will try.
I'll stop, think what I have to give:
    on judgment sound, rely.

PALM SUNDAY

Held high the slender palm leaves wave
    as caught up in the wind;
the crowds with raucous joy behave,
    Hosannas loud ascend.

"Hosanna to the King of kings,"
    they shout as with one voice.
Throughout Jerusalem there rings:
    "Hosanna!" All rejoice.

While Jesus on a donkey rides
    toward tragic Roman fate,
the atmosphere the fate now hides,
    but joy will turn to hate.

Hosannas will not satisfy.
    Within a week the crowd
is shouting boldly, "Crucify!"
    so boisterously loud.

This humble man upon an ass
    knew well what was to come,
and could but hope his death would pass
    and love would be its sum.

And so, it was upon the cross
    two words there came alive:
Forgive and *love*, our gain not loss,
    through them we may survive.

GOOD FRIDAY

How can a Friday be called good,
    when it involves a death,
when on a cross that's made of wood,
    one takes his final breath?

Good, no one then had called that day.
    Hosannas no one sang.
There left he was, all went away,
    upon the cross to hang.

Did Pontius Pilate have the thought:
    "This day is good indeed.
Perhaps my last conflict I've fought,
    and now all will concede,

"concede for Jews there is no king,
    except as reigns in Rome?
There's no Messiah, no offspring
    throughout the realm to roam."

When did "Good Friday" gain this name
    for someone's dying day?
The morn of Easter sealed its fame
    for all who came to say:

The death of Jesus on the cross,
    his open, empty tomb,
affirm that death is not a loss;
    one's death is not one's doom.

EASTER FAITH

A linen cloth, an empty tomb,
    are these signs Christ was there?
Some have their reasons, and assume
    the tomb was simply bare.

"How could it be that Christ arose?"
    some ask with good intent.
They probe the doctrines they oppose:
    with doubts sincerely meant.

Yet, hope lives on that Christ arose,
    in each believing soul,
and sacrificial love us shows
    the faith that makes us whole.

If Easter faith we would possess,
    let doubts each year depart;
self-giving love let us profess
    in every beating heart.

Chapter 5

THE STRUGGLE TO BELIEVE IN THE MYSTERY

AT THE TABLE

We're here again to share the bread,
to drink the wine Christ's love has spread.
Transformed we are who here will dine
on love, found here in bread and wine.

The love we find is to be shared,
and nothing is with it compared.
It's for the humble, rich, the poor,
and all may of this love be sure.

But we must also be a sign
and show this love is yours and mine.
We too must love the rich and poor;
that's how they'll know God's love is sure.

If love is sure, then it endures,
forever mine, forever yours.
This at the table we will learn:
God's love within our hearts must burn!

THE MYSTERY OF BREAD AND WINE

Communion bread and wine are blessed,
    the Holy Spirit's choice;
in them forgiving love's expressed
    to give each soul a voice:

A voice to share the love received
    through this, Christ's sacred meal;
a love, if trusted and believed,
    has grace and power to heal.

It heals divisions, anger, hate;
    it is a balm for strife.
It can all prejudice abate,
    give purpose to our life.

We who receive the bread and wine
    the mystery will know:
for love transforms us as we dine,
    and as we rise and go.

TO DINE WITH CHRIST

We come each week, the table spread
    with sacred bread and wine,
to dine with Christ who is our Head
    and of the church divine.

It is one holy, sacred trust
    this table to convene,
"Remember me," Christ said, we must
    in moments calm, serene.

The holy catholic church here comes
    in humble spirit bowed
to gain the strength of love which sums
    up faith it has avowed.

To dine with Christ, Savior and Lord
    of past and what will be
unites the church in one accord,
    the Holy Trinity.

HOLY SACRAMENT AND WORD

The Holy Sacrament and Word,
concepts conjoined, not to be blurred.
The word in sacrament is found;
the sacrament with word is bound.

Both for the church are sacrament,
the gift of God's divine intent.
The eucharistic life's the sum
of all we in the church become.

Our mission and our purpose too
through bread and wine, we keep in view.
Through them the sacred word is known
and seeds for serving others sown.

O HOLY SACRAMENT DIVINE

    O Holy Sacrament divine,
    adoring hearts to Christ incline,
on wings of song through ages long
    we hear the echoes of his voice:
    Come, dine with me and here rejoice!

    Rejoice, this sacrament receive,
    in sacrificial love believe,
and pray God's grace to bless each place
    where hymns of bread and wine are sung
    by young and old in every tongue.

    O Holy Sacrament divine,
    with joy now fill this heart of mine!
On wings of song through ages long
    inviting echoes of Christ's voice
    Repeat the theme: Come, dine: Rejoice!

WORD AND SACRAMENT

Link mission with the Word
    but not the sacrament!
Theology absurd
    that Christians should lament!

"REMEMBER ME"

"Remember me," the Master said
    "when sharing in this meal,"
and yet his own disciples fled.
    What happened to their zeal?
Even Peter, later called a saint,
    three times the Christ denied.
When threatened, Peter's faith grew faint,
    from Christ he turned aside.

The faithful twelve soon disappeared
    after the Master's plea;
for their own fate each one had feared,
    forgot: "Remember me."
Today we hear "Remember me,"
    when we come to commune.
But do we like his followers flee,
    to faith become immune?

Here at the table we must ask,
    Am I better than they?
And am I equal to the task,
    to hear the Master say,
"Remember me" in bread and wine,
    remember what I say,
not only when you with me dine,
    "Remember me" each day.

Chapter 6

The Struggle to Believe in the Church

YOUR CHURCH? MY CHURCH? GOD'S CHURCH?

Christ's body, scriptures call the church;
    "in Christ we all are one,"
and yet denominations search
    alone to claim God's Son.

As though God has lost all control
    of unity divine,
denominations troll and troll
    and claim, the church is mine.

Since God's church is my own to claim,
    how sad others don't see
that they on God bring only shame,
    because they can't agree.

What do you think of this bold thought:
    We know better than God
that all God's people must be taught
    which churches are a fraud?

If God's thoughts indeed aren't our own,
    as scriptures boldly claim,
what church will dare to stand alone
    all others to defame?

"Forgive! They know not what they do,"
    said Jesus from the cross.
These words are meant for churches too.
    Ignore them, what a loss!

The church is God's own mystery,
    the church alone God knows.
Throughout all human history
    church folly always shows.

THE CHURCH?

The church, how shall one it define?
The definition, is it mine?
Some human beings think they know
precisely when they must say, "No!"
to definitions not like theirs,
no matter if another cares
to pray for all to understand.
The church is God's, ruled by no band,
no band that to the church lays claim
and on all others places blame—
the blame for having missed the mark,
while they're the ones left in the dark.
The church is God's, is that so strange?
Who has the right to shape its change?
Denominations all presume,
denominations all assume
the name of "church" they all fulfill
according surely to God's will.
I wonder if God is surprised—
they're all of holy will apprised.
"In heaven God just sits and laughs."*
'Tis thus the Psalmist God's word drafts.
Church fights must be the reason why?
If so, God's "laugh" may change to "cry."

---

* Psalm 2:4.

THE CHURCH IS GOD'S?

How can some folk pray, "Make us one,"
    yet would the church divide?
They pray to Father, Spirit, Son,
    but oneness put aside.

They pray, "Thanks be to God. Amen."
    But why should they thank God,
when they again and yet again
    on unity have trod?

What blasphemy to pray this prayer:
    "Lord, make us one," we pray,
when there is no intent to share
    in unity today!

In brokenness, the church must pray:
    "Forgive our selfish thought.
The church is God's, not ours to sway
    till it's with schism fraught."

THE CHURCH WITHOUT WALLS?

A church without walls, is it church?
    "The buildings truly matter not,"
some say who for new meaning search
    beyond what's often taught.

Yet, architecture plays a role
    in how we oft respond.
We sit, we kneel, we are made whole;
    we see, we feel the bond.

The bond that's formed twixt God and all
    who worship in a space,
designed with thought, each pane, each wall,
    to seek anew God's grace.

"The house of God," is what some say
    is what we call this place,
where earnestly we come to pray
    to seek our God's embrace.

Church walls a refuge, yes, may be
    for those unjustly wronged.
'Tis then the walls offer a plea:
    "Let justice be prolonged."

Within the walls the church survives,
    but not because of walls.
They're but a symbol of the lives
    that rise when all else falls.

Yes, people are what forms the church,
    who trust in God alone;
Within, without the walls they search,
    without end the Unknown.

HUMILITY IN THE CHURCH

Humility within the church
    is sometimes hard to find.
How strange one there for it must search.
    Have humble there declined?

The humble know not who they are;
    they are not self-aware?
Humility one's sure to mar
    when it's *one's own* affair!

Humility leaves not aside
    conviction or truth's quest.
And yet, it never will deride
    sincerity expressed.

The meek will inherit the earth;
    the proud surely will not.
What then can pride to us be worth?
    False pride is all for naught.

The humble think of others first,
    even when they could be wrong,
and Christians oft are at their worst—
    trying to get along.

A CHURCH, A MOSQUE, A SYNAGOGUE

A church, a mosque, a synagogue
    are signs people seek God.
Should they be signs of dialogue,
    or signs that we are flawed?

A house of God should be a place,
    where no one seeks ill will,
with doors wide open to each race,
    where love each soul can fill.

Faith's not for careless worshipers;
    faith seeks goodwill for all.
But faith needs love interpreters;
    faith seeks no one's downfall.

A faith sincere one must admire,
    an honest quest for God,
without prejudgment or desire
    to call such faith a fraud.

UNITY—DISUNITY

When churches speak of unity
    and members disagree,
these words break down community:
    "You must agree with me."

When churches speak of love and care
    for all of humankind,
but cause disruption and despair,
    what do they have in mind?

All unity depends upon
    the art of compromise.
Without it, discord's sure to spawn,
    and unity's hope dies.

Yet compromise cannot replace
    respect and love for all.
Their absence is a dire disgrace,
    the church's worst pitfall.

If God is love, as Scripture claims,
    and loves all humankind,
the highest of the church's aims:
    let love all peoples bind.

Though love, God's love, can bind all hearts
    in unity supreme,
when churches are but warring parts,
    then unity's a dream.

www.ingramcontent.com/pod-product-compliance
Lightning Source LLC
Chambersburg PA
CBHW071733040426
42446CB00012B/2335